To all my nieces and nephews

—L.J.

I've Seen the Promised Land
The Life of Dr. Martin Luther King, Jr.
Text copyright © 2004 by Walter Dean Myers   Illustrations copyright © 2004 by Leonard Jenkins
Manufactured in China by South China Printing Company Ltd.
All rights reserved. www.harperchildrens.com

Library of Congress Cataloging-in-Publication Data
Myers, Walter Dean, 1937–
   I've seen the promised land : the life of Dr. Martin Luther King, Jr. / by Walter Dean Myers ;
illustrated by Leonard Jenkins. — 1st ed.
      p.   cm.
   Summary: Pictures and easy-to-read text introduce the life of civil rights leader Dr. Martin Luther King, Jr.
   ISBN 0-06-027703-3 — ISBN 0-06-027704-1 (lib. bdg.)
   1. King, Martin Luther, Jr., 1929–1968—Juvenile literature. 2. African Americans—Biography—Juvenile
literature. 3. Civil rights workers—United States—Biography—Juvenile literature. 4. Baptists—United
States—Clergy—Biography—Juvenile literature. 5. African Americans—Civil rights—History—20th
century—Juvenile literature. [1. King, Martin Luther, Jr., 1929–1968. 2. Civil rights workers. 3. Clergy. 4. Civil
rights movements—History. 5. African Americans—Biography.] I. Title: I have seen the promised land.
II. Jenkins, Leonard, ill. 3. Title.
E185.97.K5M936 2004   2003004098
323'.092—dc21   CIP
                                                                                                                AC

Typography by Matt Adamec   1 2 3 4 5 6 7 8 9 10   ❖   First Edition

I've Seen the Promised Land

The Life of Dr. Martin Luther King, Jr.

by Walter Dean Myers • illustrated by Leonard Jenkins

HARPERCOLLINSPUBLISHERS

 Amistad

BRING THE TROOPS HOME NOW!

I WON'T FIGHT IN VIETNAM

March 1968. The country was torn by turmoil. There were protests against racial injustice. On college campuses young men and women were opposing the long war in Vietnam.

Dr. Martin Luther King, Jr., looked at the small mountain of mail on his secretary's desk. He knew there would be requests for him to speak at schools and churches from people who loved and respected him. There would also be ugly letters full of threats and hatred.

Dr. King had been invited to Memphis, Tennessee, where sanitation workers were on strike. He was tired, but he felt he had to offer his support. Dr. King could not enjoy his own good fortune, even though he had worked hard for it, as long as there was poverty anywhere in the world.

Martin Luther King, Jr., was born in Atlanta, Georgia, on January 15, 1929. His father was one of the most respected ministers in Atlanta. But Atlanta was part of the segregated South, and young Martin had to put up with the pain of being judged by the color of his skin. He worked hard in school and became a minister. He was eager to spread the word of God's love for all people.

Then on December 1, 1955, an event occurred in Montgomery, Alabama, that would make many demands on him but also give him the opportunity to seek justice for all Americans.

The laws in Montgomery said that whites would sit in the front of the buses, and blacks in the rear. If all the front seats were taken, then any blacks who had seats would have to give them up.

One evening a woman named Rosa Parks, returning home
after a hard day's work, refused to give up her seat. She was
arrested for breaking the laws.

In response to Mrs. Parks's arrest, the black people of Montgomery planned to boycott the city buses. They said they would not pay money to ride buses if they had to give up their seats just because they were not white people.

At that time Dr. King was the pastor of the Dexter Avenue Baptist Church in Montgomery. People were so impressed with the young minister that they asked him to lead the boycott. Dr. King knew that leading a boycott would be difficult and perhaps even dangerous. But he believed that individuals had the responsibility of making democracy work.

There were groups that would do anything to stop black people from being treated as equals. Local police arrested Dr. King just to harass him, and a firebomb was thrown onto the porch of his house. This evil act frightened the young minister, but he didn't back down. He believed so strongly in the cause of justice that he had to do what was right, even if his life was at risk. His wife, Coretta Scott King, had a small baby to care for, but she supported her husband's decision.

MONTGOM
LA
UNCONSTI

The boycott lasted over a year. Finally, in June 1956, the District
Court of the United States ruled that laws separating whites and
blacks on the Montgomery buses were unconstitutional.

This ruling was later affirmed by the Supreme Court. Finally the buses in Montgomery were integrated. Blacks and whites, supported by the law, would ride together in peace.

The Montgomery bus boycott was one of the most important events in the civil rights movement. It showed that people could make changes in a system that had lasted for decades if they had the right leadership. Martin Luther King, Jr., recognized as that kind of leader, was arrested again and again as he protested the laws and practices that hurt his people. The arrests did not stop his activity or his determination. Being in prison was hard, but it was a difficulty that Dr. King gladly accepted because he knew what he was doing was right.

In 1959 Dr. King spent a month in India studying the techniques of nonviolent protest practiced by the great Indian leader Mohandas Gandhi. Dr. King had studied Gandhi's life and had taken his philosophy of nonviolence into his own heart.

Many blacks were disappointed with Dr. King's belief in nonviolence and love for all people. Some argued that blacks didn't need people to love, they needed justice. In the South black protests and attempts at integration were met with beatings and jailings. It was clear that those who opposed equal rights for blacks did not mind using violence.

While Dr. King spoke throughout the United States of nonviolence, there were others with different ideas. One of them was a man known as Malcolm X.

"Whoever heard of a nonviolent revolution?" Malcolm X asked.

But Dr. King knew that people would come to understand and respect one another only through love, not force.

The movement for justice, for bringing all people together, took many forms. In the South Dr. King led nonviolent marches. He insisted that those who worked with him practice nonviolence even though he acknowledged that it was not always an easy path to follow.

Sometimes, in Northern cities, young people exploded with anger. Dr. King understood their impatience but did not think that violence could ever turn back the winds of hatred.

By 1963 the voices of those who were against nonviolence grew louder. President John F. Kennedy seemed sympathetic to the black cause, but blacks across the country were becoming discouraged as the hostility against them increased. Night after night, news broadcasts carried stories of people being beaten, assaulted with fire hoses, and bitten by dogs as they stood up for equality. Dr. King refused to be drawn into the hatred that was directed against him. He insisted on loving his enemies and conducting the struggle of black America on the high plane of dignity and discipline.

In August 1963 a March on Washington was planned. Hundreds of thousands of people, black and white, from around the country and around the world gathered in the nation's capital to protest the wrongs in our society. It was here that Dr. King delivered his famous "I Have a Dream" speech. He spoke of a dream in which the sons of slaves and the sons of slave owners could sit down together at the table of brotherhood. He spoke of a day when his four little children would be judged not by the color of their skin, but by the content of their character.

On that hot summer day, thousands of Americans expressed their heartfelt desire for fairness and justice. It was a glorious day for America.

On September 15, 1963, less than a month after the March on Washington, a bomb blast shattered the early morning stillness in Birmingham, Alabama. When the smoke cleared, four black girls lay dead in the rubble of the Sixteenth Street Baptist Church. It was the kind of brutality against which Dr. King had always spoken.

The country mourned as Dr. King declared that the four girls had not died in vain. Tears were shed as he called them heroines in the struggle for freedom and human dignity. But for many the forces of evil seemed to have the upper hand. Then, in November 1963, the president of the United States, John F. Kennedy, was assassinated. Violence seemed to rule the country.

Dr. King maintained his course. He had been jailed. His life had been threatened. Bombs had been thrown at his house. Still he carried on. People asked him how long he could carry on in the face of growing brutality. How long? How long?

The question tormented Dr. King, but he had faith that hatred could not last forever. He still believed that justice would rise up from the ashes of despair and that those who held out for love would one day prevail.

In 1964 Dr. Martin Luther King, Jr., received the Nobel Peace Prize in recognition of his great work.

Over the next few years Dr. King watched in sorrow as anger roared through the streets of our nation's cities.

In 1965 Malcolm X became another victim of violence, brutally murdered as he spoke to those he hoped to help.

Dr. King understood that it sometimes seemed right to tear down a society that simply would not listen to the reason of justice, but he knew that one day justice would win out over evil.

In the spring of 1968, Dr. King had been asked to support the striking sanitation workers in Memphis. Just days before his arrival, there were signs that the promised peaceful protest would be hard to control. Dr. King was discouraged, but he put aside his feelings. He thought that if he put himself before the people, they would remain calm.

On March 28 Dr. King led a march through downtown Memphis. The anger that the sanitation workers felt boiled over into the streets. The result was, for Dr. King, a disaster. One young man was killed and fifty others were injured. Dr. King wondered if his message had fallen on deaf ears.

On April 3, 1968, at the Masonic Temple in Memphis, Dr. King spoke of his life. He said that he had been to the mountaintop and seen the promised land. He knew he might not reach that land with his people. But still he held on to the faith that America would become the promised land of liberty and justice for all.

The next evening, on April 4, Dr. King stood on the balcony of the Lorraine Motel. Suddenly a shot rang out. Dr. King fell backward. The man who preached nonviolence had been murdered.

Dr. King knew that there would be a day when he would die, and he knew he might die a violent death. Yet Dr. King's legacy lives with all of us. His example stands as a glowing light for us to follow. And it is to the mountaintop of idealism, and of hope for justice, that we look to find his image still.

Dr. King wanted to be remembered simply as someone who had tried to do his best and to serve all people, regardless of race. He wanted to be remembered as someone who believed in love, who believed in peace. He wanted to be remembered as someone who did not turn away from those who were hungry, or those in prison. And so we remember him as a man, as a leader, and as a father. We look to him as a man who tried to keep our country on the righteous path to freedom and equality.

Chronology of Civil Rights Movement

January 15, 1929	Martin Luther King, Jr., is born.
May 17, 1954	Brown v. Board of Education of Topeka: Supreme Court ruling desegregates classrooms in twenty-one states.
December 1, 1955	Rosa Parks keeps her bus seat in Montgomery, Alabama.
December 21, 1956	Buses in Montgomery, Alabama, are integrated.
August 28, 1963	Dr. King gives "I Have a Dream" speech at March on Washington, D.C.
September 15, 1963	Church bombing in Birmingham, Alabama.